The Pleasure, Pain and Beauty of a Woman's

Life Journey

Angelic "The Light" Renee

All Poems Written By Angelic Renee

Copyright © 2016 All Rights Reserved

Greetings Kings & Queens,

I am so grateful that you purchased my poetry book! And I hope you find at least one poem in my book that makes you think, feel motivated, inspired or just simply entertains you. I've been writing since 1999 and finally decided to let go of fear, and share just a few of my most personal poems based on my life, I've written over the years and recently. Putting this book together has been one of the most spiritual and cleansing experiences I've had in a while, this book was part of my closure and healing of many wounds I still had open. I feel blessed that God gave me the gift of writing and I encourage you to use any spiritual gifts and talents, you are blessed with as well, use it before you lose it! Blessings to you readers and please continue to support my art in the future if you enjoy this piece. Peace and Love ♥

Table Of Contents

- The Monster In My Room
- I Forgive You (For My Father)
- Tempted To A Point
- How Can I Sleep
- Hip-Hop
- Jam With Me
- More Than Pussy
- World Wide Web
- Religion
- Mask
- Tell Me
- Mourning
- Stay Home
- Practice
- Alone
- Just Wanted To Be Loved
- Untitled (For David)
- Your Loving
- What Happened To Your Light
- Skin War
- She's Dead
- Woman

This Book is Dedicated to & In The Memory of

Renee and Michael

Monster In My Room   2016

When we were kids we were told to look out for the monsters in our room

That hid under our beds or in our closet

Cover our faces with our blankets and close our eyes real tight

For they only come out in the night

Till this day I still sleep with some kind of light on

I use to love scary movies until they became my reality

Memories of the shadow on the walls replay in my mind

I repressed the monster for years but visions returned through time

My mother always told me never to let any strangers touch me on my privates

But she didn't tell me what to do if it wasn't a stranger

I was in danger in my own home

Sleeping comfortably on my bunk bed

I felt a hand part my legs, I became instantly filled with fear and rage

The rubbing on my secret spot felt like a nightmare

I began to toss and turn, pretending I was still asleep

Was this the monster they warned me about

I told myself the next time it happened, I would be brave enough to open my eyes and look at the monster in the dark

I was only five or six but I knew this wasn't right

When I built up the courage to look, I realized I knew the monster by name

I tried to tell my mother what had happened

But the fear in her eyes scared me into silence

She grabbed me by my shirt shouting "Angie, did something happen!!!?

I replied "Never mind Mommy, it was just a dream"

How long this went on for, how far did this go, I will never know

I am glad the brain blocks out most traumatic experiences

I wonder if my mother knew deep down inside, but was too afraid to face the truth

Even though I forgave her

I will never forget The Monster In My Room.

I Forgive You (For My Father) 2016

You were the first man I loved and the first to break my heart

Because of you I chased the wrong men for years

Trying to make them love me, proving I was worthy

I didn't even know you affected me, until I realized, all my relationships were with men, who didn't love me or abused me

My mother over loved me to make up for you not being there

But her love couldn't heal the fact my father didn't care

The days I would sit at the window waiting for you to pick me up

From sun rise to sun set you would never show up

You were considered the cool uncle and a father figure to neighborhood kids

But where was your love for your own kid?

I was shocked when my mother told me you named me

It was a burden to carry your last name growing up

You didn't have a relationship with your own father so maybe psychologically that also messed you up

I endured fatherless birthdays, graduations and first moments

I have your eyes, your size, your hands and feet

Did the anger from my mother divorcing you make you punish me?

When you did pick me up, you would drop me off to friends, lovers, your sister or mother's

Running from fatherhood

You were usually drunk or high when I saw you

When you were sober you were kind and sweet, would over feed me and tell me I was beautiful

We had this little saying " Who loves daddy"? I would reply "Angelic " and you would give me multiple kisses on the cheek

Then you would disappear for months on end

Leaving me gasping for my father's love like air

I was eighteen when you got on your hands and knees and begged for my forgiveness

I told you I didn't forgive you, and I was too old now for you to teach me anything new

You cried and I cried and the next time I saw you was at your funeral

The day you died I knew It inside, my phone rang nonstop all day, I hoped it was your mother instead

Only one tear dropped when I heard the words "Michael is dead "

I was numb with anger and pain; how could you die on me? I didn't get a chance to make you pay!?

Your funeral was in the morning and I was my mother's maid of honor that night

Till this day I feel unhuman for getting through that moment

I paid for your wake with the death benefit, your mother kept the insurance money and stole the Mercedes Benz, the only thing that you left me

Three years later my mother was dead and for some reason God sent me to live with your mother instead

That's when I learned the truth, you were raised by a demon, how could you know love, *it wasn't given to you?*

Not making excuses for your behavior, but I understand now

If she treated and spoke to me like I was lower than the ground, I can imagine what she did to you

I use to wonder how could you call her out of her name

After living with her, I wonder how we were so strong not to physically harm her

You were the black sheep and your sister the golden child

When you died I became your narcissistic mother's new supply

She never spoke good things about you, kept only two photos of you, tucked away in a dusty corner

Telling me for years I wouldn't be shit "You are just like your father"

I wish you could have healed before you passed

Maybe we had much more in common than we knew

I started my own business and I am a hustler just like you

The land you owned your car wash on was sold and I never saw a dime

No need to seek revenge because every sinner must serve their time

The best part of the story is I'm no longer blue about you

Because God healed me and showed me the truth

Sometimes parents aren't perfect and weren't raised right, so before you hate them, take a look at your family's tree

I forgave myself

I forgave my father

I forgave my grandmother

Forgiveness set me free!

Tempted To A Point   2002

Every day I walk into them

Yeah that's right, the "older man" or the "old head" as they say

They stop me in the street looking me dead in my face

It doesn't matter which race they are, they are all the same

And they say " Hey pretty girl, what is your name?

Do you have man or Can I have your number?

I know that they can see I'm much younger

Yet they still have intensions to be with me, in other words, sleeping with me is on their agenda

Yes, I am mature for my age, but I don't look beyond my days

Mr. 1969, yeah you're fine

They say to me "Where have you been all my life "?

I reply in mind "Trying to be born, fool"!

Why do older men think messing with little girls is cool?

But damn at the same time, I'm tempted by the experience they have and the moves they could show me

After a while their charm grows on me

I'm starting to like the way they guide me and control me

Visions in my mind in how the intimacy would be

Pause I'm moving too fast, trying to be a grown ass

I enjoyed the rush but the temptation must stop

Mama warned me about these types, this isn't right

In the end all I will be left with, is emotional pain

While feeding their sexual needs and manhood is their only gain.

How Can I Sleep? 2009

How can I sleep when there's things to be done?

How can I sleep when there's dreams to achieve?

How can I sleep when I have to fish just to eat?

I'm up while the world sleeps peacefully because they have

I'm plotting, thinking, planning on how to survive when the sun comes up

How can I sleep when I'm forced to hustle?

How can I sleep when my ends haven't met?

Struggle equals insomnia

Tell me how can I sleep when I'm in need?

Hip-Hop (Inspired by Brown Sugar)   2002

Hip-Hop is me

Hip-Hop is within me

Hip-Hop are my people

I love Hip-Hop

I dream Hip-Hop

I smell Hip-Hop

I watch Hip-Hop grow

Listening on my radio & watching videos

I dress Hip-Hop

I walk Hip-Hop

I speak to Hip-Hop and It speaks back to me

Mind, Body and Soul

Beat boxing in the Bronx, breaking dancing in the park

Battling on the street corner

Word Up, Right On, Source, VIBE magazines

That keeps Hip Hop alive

Let me explain, Hip Hop is not all about the bling-bling, cars, Cristal, cash and ass

It's about the first time you heard Rapper's Delight

When you realized Rick was Slick

That feeling you get when B.I.G comes on in the club

The way LL licks his lips

Ladies backing that ass up to Juvenile

Now that's Hip Hop

Hip Hop is me

Hip Hop is within me

Hip Hop helped shape me

From Adidas to Air force ones

Gold herringbone to pure platinum chains

vinyl, cassettes and cd's

Kangols to fitteds

Hip-Hop has become a mission

A mission of unity, a mission of love

When I hear Hip-Hop I can't help but to node my head

My headphones on blast, zoning to Jigga man

Hip-Hop is not phony

Hip Hop is Real

Hip -Hop is a something that you feel

Hip-Hop is about being you and being free

Now tell me...

When did you first fall in love with Hip-Hop? ♥

Jam With Me (Until)   2012

Those lips, those eyes

The main reason you get me to spread my thighs

Your lines finger pop my mind

Just in time for your tongue's magic show

I soar as you explore

Hands taking a tour

Chills running from crown to my feet

With every stroke my soul moans, and my body whispers "Give me more"

Your thickness is soothing and healing

I'm dizzy from your scent

Lost in your positions and consistence

Yet there's still something missing

Our rhythm, our beat, our song

Lyrics, bass, blues, funk, dance

Not saying the loving isn't good baby

Just maybe it will feel different if I was your lady

When you're able to say you love me

Can't live without me

No doubts, no fears, no walls

All emotions

Until then I'll pretend and continue to enjoy, this body rocking, earth shaking, room vibrating penetration, you only offer me

But for how long will that be?

More Than Pussy   2006

What am I projecting to men is in questioning

Could it be the way I walk in a room?

I swear I never sway my hips, barely ever lick my lips

Yet they wanna pound between my big thighs till I cry, claiming "It's all your fault, you made it rise"

I rather they not lust, put a pause to their dirty thoughts

Society rejects me, because of my obesity

While some men openly seduce me

Should I change my style?

Stop the staring, groaning, whistling and hollering

For once look me in the eyes

Then you will see

 I'm worth much more than just some good ole pussy

World Wide Web   2016

My imagination has always got me into trouble

Every man I made love to in my mind, manifested in the physical

But with you it's different

I don't imagine sexual fantasies about you

My thoughts run deeper and that's what frightens me

Because we never met in the physical body

Only in what I call the matrix

The world wide Web

Web of lies

Somehow makes you feel connected to perfect strangers

The internet seems to be an illusion

We only show what we want others to see

Why does it seem like you're not trying to be impressive?

Or have I just created you into a man that I want you to be

When I think of you, I vision us sharing ideas and dreams

Of course with kisses in between

I tell myself you're not real

Just an image behind a screen

I have my life and you have yours

We probably wouldn't click in person

Or would we?

I will admire you from a distance

Attracted to your mind or at least the character you play

You feel close yet so far away

When the time is right

We'll meet face to face

Maybe just maybe

Never mind.... I'm just going to keep liking your social media posts, until you notice me

Because that's how this generation communicates

When I see you on the news feed, I get a rush

I guess I can call you my cyber crush

Oh how the World Wide Web, can play with your heart and your head

Imagination.

Religion   2016

Raised and baptized in the Seventh Day Adventist faith

When I told people I was Adventist they would say "I didn't know you practiced witchcraft"

I didn't get it, until I researched the past

Was told to believe, never told why I should

Guilt, shame and fear was placed on me for control

People thought my family was perfect, but they had no idea what went on at home

He was an elder and she was a deaconess

Their marriage was defiled with harlots in the church, who willingly for a married man, would lift up their dress

When she turned to the church for help, they turned their back on her

So she ran to the Baptist faith out of hurt

Religion

I always had a connection and understanding of God

even from a young age

He gave me end times dreams and visions before things would happen

When I began to see pure spirits and demons

My brothas and sistas told me, I was crazy and needed medication

It took me a long time to realize I was chosen

And that they are the blind, unable to see out of their third eye

Hopefully they will be able to see soon, because we are running out of time

Religion

Most of my friends in the church were having sex by 13, today a lot of them have multiple baby mamas & daddies and working on their second marriage before 30

Dated an Adventist pastor, he broke up with me because I wouldn't give it up, did me worse than a non-believer you would meet in the club

Religion

Sometimes when I listen to people speak

They seem to be in love with the building and not the Father

I don't need a middle man to connect to Yahweh

No pope, confessionals, no pastors, only my Creator

Religion

When I left the Adventist faith I went to multiple churches searching for God when all along He was inside me

Landed in a Baptist church

Asked to give 4 offerings and tithes

I don't mind giving, but dang, what will I have left to stay alive ?

You better shout or praise dance or they'll think the devil lives inside

Pastor's swinging his wrists from side to side as he's preaching, he's staring at men in the front row with lustful eyes

How can you lead us with a sodomite mind?

Religion

People think I need to go to the altar

Just because I'm not in the front row

Doesn't mean I don't believe in God the Father, The Son and The Holy Ghost

I'm closer to God than I've ever been in my life

It breaks my heart when people in leadership tell me

"I've never heard His voice"

I read the Bible but I also have knowledge of self

If you don't know your history, your future will be mentally, emotionally and spiritually harder

So when I say I will only marry a man of God, I'm not speaking religiously

A man that doesn't put God first can never Lead me

I am not against religion It's just not a part of my calling

Without religion I finally feel free to be me

Not free to sin and be unstable

Free to listen, love, connect and be one with my God

He deserves all the praise, He's been so faithful to me

God is the Only religion if you ask me!

MASK   2016

When we met I was lost and you found me

Found me on Myspace to be exact, I tilted my head to the side staring at your photograph

I knew something was off but I ignored the red flags, because you were charming, fun and caring

Just what I needed to numb the pain I was feeling inside

since my mother died

I told you my deepest darkest secrets and you told me yours

7 years apart in age, you made me feel like a kid again, and then our ages faded as we became best friends

We made memories, that replay in my head

We were so close people thought I had you in bed, but I never touched you, even when you appeared to be more straight than gay

You named me your soul friend, gave me a ring, matching tattoos

Damn what the hell was I thinking, I had no idea I was signing a soul contract

Had to pray to God to get my soul back, because you wouldn't return it

You were taken my sanity, gas lighting me, triangulating me with fake friends and under cover lovers

I should have known something wasn't right, your "I love you" never felt right

I was more like a mother to you, I see why your real mother hates me

Maybe I gave you a love you never had, never saw growing up or knew existed

You say you want love, but you act as if love is your enemy

I stayed up late nights crying and praying for change, as you slept in another state peacefully

How the hell did you have me on a string from thousands of miles away?

But I'm an angel and I finally figured out how to use my wings

I think about what was real, what was fake

I guess I had faith light kills darkness, and my spirit can heal you

Your mask has fallen off

I wonder... who did I love, the demon or you?

Tell Me (For Mommy) 2008

Tell me what happened when you took your last breath

Did you feel your last heartbeat, were you in pain?

Was there a bright light at the end of the tunnel as they say?

What were your last thoughts and words?

Does your spirit still exist?

Or are you just resting like sleeping beauty, waiting for God to wake you up?

Can you see me, can you hear me, can you touch me, if so why can't I feel you?

Tell me where you are, what really happens after death

Come on give me a sign what's the whole meaning of life?

What portion of my heart and soul did you take, ever since you left I don't look of feel the same?

Are you in heaven?

Tell me which direction I should go, who should I love, who should I hate?

Will my baby's eyes be able to see your ghostly face?

Life or Death which shall I fear?

Tell me are you there, are you near? ♥

Mourning

2004

Over slept this morning

But then again I wasn't in any rush

Pulled out my black dress

For today I'm in mourning

Sipping on my tea slowly

Avoiding getting ready

Because I rather not go

Placing on my sunglasses

Blocking out the redness in my eyes

Taking a deep breath, before walking through the church doors

Sitting in the back row, not wanting a closer view

Watching the congregation's reaction made me even more blue

Hearing the singing built up anger inside me

Overwhelmed with emotions

Couldn't hold them inside

That's when I rose from my seat

Ran down the aisle and fell to my knees

Looked him in the eyes and said "Please don't marry her, marry me!".

Stay Home   2008

Today I will ignore the fact that I love you

I will try to forget how many years we have known each other

I will not answer your phone calls or texts

I will not vision your kisses on my neck

This time I will delete all nude photos you send through emails

Today I will not be tempted to touch myself, to the thought of wanting you

I will not give you the pleasure of making me feel guilty anymore

I will not allow you to tamper with my self-esteem and actions

Today I will not wish, it was I, who you married instead

But I will hope for a bright future for your son

I can care less how miserable you are, being married to her

She was your choice even though you knew me first

I will gain my self-respect back

I will no longer be your daily escape

I will not counsel you or pray for your happiness

Even though we didn't make love

It's the emotional part that feels so wrong

I will not be afraid to let it all go and tell you to just...

Stay Home.

Practice   2004

The alarm clock I gave you had no reason to tick

Food that I cooked should have not been ingested

Letters, poems, pictures and cards, wishing they had been lost in the mail

Late night calls

Laughter

Quality time

Every dime spent

Movies in Park Chester

Waiting for sex

Train rides on the 6

Hugs and Kisses

Compliments

Cute outfits to impress

Times I sat and thought of us

Back massages, soft and rough

Meeting friends and family

Future plans which included you

Giving up on potential lovers

Faking it to feed your ego

Black lace nighty

Exchange of dreams and fears

Defended your character with my Momma

2am cab rides over the Whitestone Bridge

Cut a few classes

Slept on the floor

Towel under the door

Inhaled your weed

Actor of the year and I the best supporting actress

I played a fool

I thought this was love

 when along, you were just Practice!

Alone   2008

I sleep alone

I eat alone

I'm home alone

I shop alone

I drink alone

I love alone

I cry alone

I worship alone

I am alone on holidays

I stand alone in this world, despite what others may think

I am in a crowded room and still stand alone

I've been alone for so long

I am immune to loneliness.

Just Wanted To Be Loved   2008

Sick and tired, of being sick and tired and being hurt

The ones you love, never love you, and the ones that love you, you can never seem to love them

Why should they love me when Daddy never did?

They just want me close to lay up in my bed

Want privileges without commitment

Will you have my baby? Such a played out line, I hear all the time

Tic-Toc, Tic-Toc

No not my biological, just the clock, reminding me of how much time I've wasted with you

Sick and tired, of being sick and tired and being hurt

You start but can't finish

I just need company, a homie, lover, friend

But I'm sure the next girl you meet, you'll marry them

So I wait around and play your games because at least I can say I'm not alone

No girl It's not you, It's me

Maybe if we met me when we were seventeen

I'm good enough to cook, clean, even be his nasty freak

Yet still no ring

I could give him head so good he'll forget his name, I can discover a new planet, he'll still treat me the same

No matter what I do, It's never good enough

Sick and tired of being sick and tired, and being hurt

I wear dark shades to cover my tears

I wear a mean face to protect my fears

So nobody will know the emotional pain, and verbal abuse I'm receiving from the man I love

The boy got my body, even worse he got my mind and soul

Didn't want to listen when Mama said "Leave him alone"

Now I'm all alone, crying out to God

For solutions and healing

How did I end up here?

When all I wanted Was To Be Loved?

(Untitled) For David   2013

He has dopiness stitched in his DNA

When he walks in a room women's nipples rise to the occasion

He is a glimpse of Boaz

He has the strength of Samson

He is my choice of intoxication

I inhale him, his energy gets me high

He is my mama's cooking on Sunday afternoon

He is my motivator, teacher, listener, encourager and prophet

He is my need, not just my want

Not afraid to tuck his shirt in his pant, and use proper grammar

He is the poster man of my future

He is what I desire my son to be like

He is my chemistry type

A man of God, a threat to Satan

His kisses are like mini tours of heaven

He's brown sugar

He's worth the wait...But damn! He said he just wants to be friends.

Your Loving   2003

Would it be wrong if I told you all I wanted was your loving?

Guess it's your fault, you got me hooked

No need for a conversation, just give me what I want

Never imagined it would be like this

I wish I could have you every day

Tell me how you feel about my loving

If you listen closely you can hear my body calling

It's obvious I'm addicted

You come correct every time you give it

That thing you do with your hand always drives me wild

Satisfying me with every stroke

After we cum, I wanna start again

Never feeling bored

Our favorite spot is the floor

New position after new position

Love watching you make those funny faces

Eyes shut closed as you take it real deep

Like it when you're tasting me

Kisses leaving me breathless

My breast against your smooth brown skin

Licking my legs, neck and back

Your scent alone could make me wet

Circular motions got tears dropping down my face

So fulfilling, has me on a high

Hate when it comes to an end

Can you blame me, you're the best lover I ever had?

I always enjoy

Making love to you ♥

ALMOST   2003

The Stare

The Compliment

The Response

The Wonder

The Pen & Paper

The Phone Call

The First Date

The First Kiss

The Emotions

The Love

The Fear

The Defense

The Lies

The Pain

The Tears

The Distance

The Excuses

The Apology

The Forgiveness

The Exhaustion

The Change

The End

The Void

The Memory

Almost.

What Happened To Your Light?   2015

Haven't seen you in a while boy, you're looking kinda dull boy

You're still fine but dry

When I met you, you shined brighter than the southern night skies

Tell me what happened since we parted, what turned off your light?

Did life hit you hard?

You're smiling but you aren't shining like you use to

It was your beam of light that blinded me, your voice of an angel that wooed me

Tell me boy why are you so dark?

I no longer have to wear sunglasses in your presence

You look me in the eyes, and ask to return to my dimension

Claiming when I left your life, things weren't the same

How I was your light, but my absence blew out your flame

Ignite me, Ignite me

 You beg for my light

But this time I won't light a match

My light's too bright to play in the dark.

Skin War   2016

Light skin versus dark skin

A worldwide catastrophe

That even the Asians are using bleaching creams

The effects of slavery run deeply through my people's veins

Chains are off our hands and feet, but still on our brains

Time has not changed anything

It's still the field salve and house salve against one another, as if we had control in choosing our skin color

My light skin is a constant reminder, that my great grandmothers were raped

It is not a badge of honor for me to be lighter

I am told I have privileges and I admit I'm still looking for the benefits

Because according to the white man I'm still a nigga b*tch

If slavery started all over again, we would all be in chained together

Get to know me first before you assume, I think I am better

I would never know If they hired me for my abilities, Caucasian safe name or my lighter skin

"Stop acting light skin" my brothas shout at me

Have you ever thought maybe I'm rejecting you, because you're simply not the man for me?

Growing up I didn't feel black enough, so I use to over compensate

Would relax my natural curly hair to be bone straight

So I can fit in with the other black girls, rocking a dubi wrap

Black girls would constantly say "You're not black"

But my black parents, wide black nose and black behind told me otherwise

"He only likes you, because you look mixed"

Even had a friend nick name me "piss"

Is it better to be more accepted by the Caucasians, and rejected from your own nation?

So I'm not black enough?

Was Malcolm, Rosa, Huey, Angela, Adam Clayton not black enough too?

I'm not saying I know the pain and struggle of a darker person

But why must we colorize each other like a living breathing Willie Lynch letter

Black people act as if light skin and dark skin are two different races

Let's teach our sons and daughters to love the skin that they're in

We hate ourselves, while the world steals from us, and pays thousands to look like us

Our melanin is power that they wish they could bottle up

Embrace your dark skin

It's evidence of God, Earth, the Sun and that we are Magic!

It's so bad that when people see celebrities with a light skin woman

Our own people say " Damn couldn't he have chosen a real black woman"?

I use to pretend I was Dominican because at least I could blend in

That didn't last long since I don't speak the language

"Why aren't you speaking Spanish, you're too pretty to be black "?

I almost mentally didn't come back from that

Just because some of us are lighter, doesn't mean we haven't been hurt too

Afflicting your pain on to your own people is insane

We are the first civilization, yet the first to tear ourselves down

This light skin versus dark skin war needs to come to an end in our minds

Weren't centuries of slavery enough time?

We don't have the power to change others, the change starts from self

Let's create our own standards of beauty

Don't let society or media tell you who you are

You are Enough and you've come this far

I am a proud black woman

That's something nobody's thoughts or words can take away from me

We are African Kings and Queens!

She's Dead   2016

I appreciate you trying to return to reminisce on what we use to have

But those are just memories of the past

To you those were good times, but when I reflect back, those were bad moments

When I didn't love myself and I settled for what men were willing to give to me

Like a thirsty traveler in the desert, in need of water, I needed men

I wasn't aware of the value of my time, my love and my body

God had to come and get me and teach me my worth

Break me in half and make me whole again

My daughter he said, I created you to be Queen, but you treat yourself as a peasant!

I had a calling on my life I wasn't answering

Spiritual gifts and talents I wasn't using

Love deficient from childhood

Because Daddy didn't love me, God was my father all that time but I was too blind to see

When you love yourself, you don't accept certain treatment from others

So sorry but not sorry If I come off different

You knew the weaker version of me

I'm strong now, in love, in faith and wisdom

We had our moment, which helped me to grow

I don't regret our connection we once had, but the woman you're missing & want back, is now dead!

Woman   2016

Wedding day talk is a part of a little girl's fantasy

Mine was moving out on my own and becoming a baby mama

I told my mother, don't worry there won't be wedding plans, just pay for my baby shower

Because in my mind a man was a waste of time

Why would I want a husband?

If all they do is cheat on you, beat on you and creep through the door late at night

My mother pretending be happy just to say she had a family

I was kid thinking to myself "That won't be me "

If I was my mother, I would be working on my third marriage at 33

We yearn for the love we never received as a child

I no longer judge my mother; she was just a product of her environment

Her four marriages weren't a success, and some people look at me as a reflection of her

I am my own woman and I broke that bondage

Took me years to heal and deal with the fact that, she and my step father weren't an image of a real marriage

God had to grab me up and tell me I was made to be a wife

I'm attracted to souls first and physical body second

He took my aggression and turned it into submission

I use to be able to have sex without emotions

Now, if I don't love you, you can't even touch my temple

Sex, nude photos or flirty talk doesn't interest me

How can a woman say she wants a husband, but is not carrying herself as a wife?

Letting men take samples of her, when she should be on reserve for the man that will crown her

I never met a married couple I admired

So one day my King and I will become our own example

I'm closer to my future husband than I've ever been before

Because I'm closer to the Woman God created me to be

Do you know how hard I prayed, healed and suffered to receive a husband?

He is getting the best version of myself

And I owe it all to the Creator for transforming me into a Woman

People ask me why do I think I'm qualified be a wife

I simply respond "I was trained for it "

God prepares you, before he blesses you

He renewed my mind and altered my life

Cleared away bad habits and removed toxic friends

When he finds me, I will be ready

I will recognize him because he will be like no other man I've experienced

It's better to wait for my God ordained mate, then to suffer like the impatient ones around me

I can now call myself a Woman

And because of this, my future husband can finally find Me! ♥

Made in United States
Orlando, FL
10 February 2024